SRA
Open
Court
Reading

Back to School

Grade 1

Mc
Graw
Hill
Education

Program Authors

Carl Bereiter, Ph.D.
Andrew Biemiller, Ph.D.
Joe Campione, Ph.D.
Doug Fuchs, Ph.D.
Lynn Fuchs, Ph.D.

Steve Graham, Ph.D.
Karen Harris, Ph.D.
Jan Hirshberg, Ed.D.
Anne McKeough, Ph.D.
Marsha Roit, Ed.D.

Marlene Scardamalia, Ph.D.
Marcy Stein, Ph.D.
Gerald H. Treadway Jr, Ph.D.

Photo Credits

4 sozaijiten/Datacraft/Getty Images; **5** ©Jose Luis Pelaez Inc/Blend Images LLC, Fancy/Alamy, KidStock/age footstock.
Back Cover: ©Jose Luis Pelaez Inc/Blend Images LLC, Fancy/Alamy, KidStock/age footstock.

Acknowledgment

Grateful acknowledgment is given to the following publishers and copyright owners for permissions granted to reprint selections from their publications. All possible care has been taken to trace ownership and secure permission for each selection included. In case of any errors or omissions, the Publisher will be pleased to make suitable acknowledgments in future editions.

First published in the United States under the title FIRST GRADE STINKS! by Mary Ann Rodman, illustrated by Beth Spiegel. Text Copyright © 2006 by Mary Ann Rodman. Illustrations Copyright © 2006 by Beth Spiegel. Published by arrangement with Peachtree Publishers.

MHEonline.com

Send all inquiries to:
McGraw-Hill Education
8787 Orion Place
Columbus, OH 43240

ISBN: 978-0-07-669818-9
MHID: 0-07-669818-1

Printed in the United States of America.

1 2 3 4 5 6 7 8 9 QLM 21 20 19 18 17 16

Table of Contents

BIG Idea

Why do we go to school?

Theme Connections

What are these students learning?

Background Builder Video
connected.mcgraw-hill.com

First Grade Stinks!

by Mary Ann Rodman
illustrated by Beth Spiegel

"First day, first grade!" I sing. "Can't wait, can't wait." "We're big kids now, Haley," says my friend Ryan as we get off the bus.

Little kids stand at the school door, holding their parents' hands. Not Ryan and me. We walk into school all by ourselves.

"Hi, Ms. Lacy," we call to our teacher from last year.
"Hello, Haley and Ryan."

Ms. Lacy's shirt is the color of daffodils. Her sneakers match. Inside her room, the dragon kite still hangs from the ceiling. Cutouts of leaves cover the wall.

Kindergartners push through the door.

"Kindergartners don't know how to act," I say.

"Poor little kindergartners," Ryan says. "We first graders know how to act."

We find our new room. Our
teacher's shirt is the color of dead
leaves. She wears ugly brown sandals.

"Good morning," she says. "My name
is Ms. Gray. Find the desk with your
name on it." She gives us a tiny smile.
Not a sunny-morning smile like
Ms. Lacy's.

This room does not look like
Ms. Lacy's. Nothing hangs from the
ceiling. Nothing on the walls. Just the
alphabet letters over the chalkboard.

No kite.
No colors.
No fun.

Ms. Gray calls the roll.

"Ryan…"
"Here!"

"Erika…"
"Here!"

"Kirk……"
"Yo!"

We stand by our chairs and say
who we are and what we like best.
Then Ms. Gray says, "Time to write
our A's and B's."

Sasha raises her hand. "We had
share time first in kindergarten."
Ms. Gray shakes her head.
"We are too busy for share time
right now. Ryan, please hand out
the writing paper."

No fair! Ms. Lacy always let *me* hand out the paper.

No share time?

No dragon kite?

No smiley teacher in a daffodil shirt?

First grade stinks!

Writing is very hard work. I am ready for recess.

But when the kindergarten kids march by our door on their way to first recess, Ms. Gray says, "Time for art." She passes around crayons and paper.

I raise my hand. "Isn't it time for recess?"

"In first grade, we have only one recess," says Ms. Gray.

I like art, but I'd rather have recess.

Ms. Gray looks at our pictures.

"Haley, what an interesting sky," she says, but not like she means it.

I like orange skies. So did Ms. Lacy.

Ms. Gray hangs Kirk's picture in front by the chalkboard. His sky is blue. I want to throw my crayons at Kirk.

"First grade stinks," I tell Ryan at recess. He blinks. "I like first grade." I want to pinch Ryan.

After recess, we write some more.
"Haley, your A's and B's are not the
same size," says Ms. Gray. "Write them
again, please."

I look at Ryan's letters. They
are exactly like the ones over
the chalkboard.

"Eyes on your own work, Haley,"
warns Ms. Gray.

First grade stinks!

Later that afternoon, Ms. Gray says, "It's story time."

Erika raises her hand. "What about naptime? In kindergarten, we had naps after lunch."

Oh no! I hate naptime!

"First graders
don't take naps,"
says Ms. Gray.

No naptime?
Maybe first grade
doesn't *always* stink.

Ms. Gray reads a story about a boy and his dog. They are lost and it's dark and then. . . . Ms. Gray closes the book!

"That's all for today. Time for math."

What happens to the boy and his dog? No fair!

Last year, Ms. Lacy read us whole books with lots of pictures all in one day. **BINKY BUG** was my favorite.

In first grade, even the stories stink.

"Can we go back to Ms. Lacy?"
I whisper to Ryan.
"Haley, no whispering,"
says Ms. Gray.
I can't stand it one more minute!

"First grade stinks!" I yell!

"First grade stinks!"

The room is very, very quiet.
Ms. Gray comes to my desk. She looks
very, very tall.

"You're in trouble now," says Ryan.

I wish Ryan would dry up and
blow away.

Ms. Gray kneels beside me. "What's wrong, Haley?"

"Writing is hard and there's only one recess and the stories don't end right," I say. "First grade stinks."

Ms. Gray smiles. It's a nice smile.
"That's not the end of the story,"
she says. "Just the end of the chapter."

"What's a chapter?" I ask.

"It's a part of a story. I'll read a chapter tomorrow and a chapter the next day. It might take a week to finish the story."

"Ms. Lacy read **BINKY BUG** all in one day," I tell her.

Ms. Gray smiles again. "In first grade we read books with chapters. Soon you'll be able to read them yourself."

"Really?" I say. "All by myself?"
Happiness whooshes inside me.
    Ms. Gray nods. "That's why
we work so hard. It's a lot to
remember, isn't it?"

time, a boy and his dog...

I smile real big. My heart glows like an orange sky.

Ms. Gray doesn't look like Ms. Lacy. Or act like Ms. Lacy. But she knows how I feel. Just like Ms. Lacy.

I can teach her to like orange skies.

Poor kindergartners.
They can't read.
They take naps.
Their books don't
have chapters.
Kindergarten stinks.

First grade is great!

The First Day of First Grade

by Milo Reese
illustrated by Nomar Perez

36

I know this building,
I have been here before.
Another school year begins
when I walk through that door.

There is so much to do!
There is so much to see!

Take a deep breath,
Count one-two-three;
Hey! Look over there!
My friends are waiting for me!

A New Friend at School

by Tanya Anderson
illustrated by Peter Francis

A new student is in my class today. My teacher needs someone to show the new student around. I want to help. I raise my hand and say, "I will."

38

I smile at the new student. Then I tell him my name. "What's your name?" I ask him. I want him to feel at home here. He smiles and says his name is Patrick.

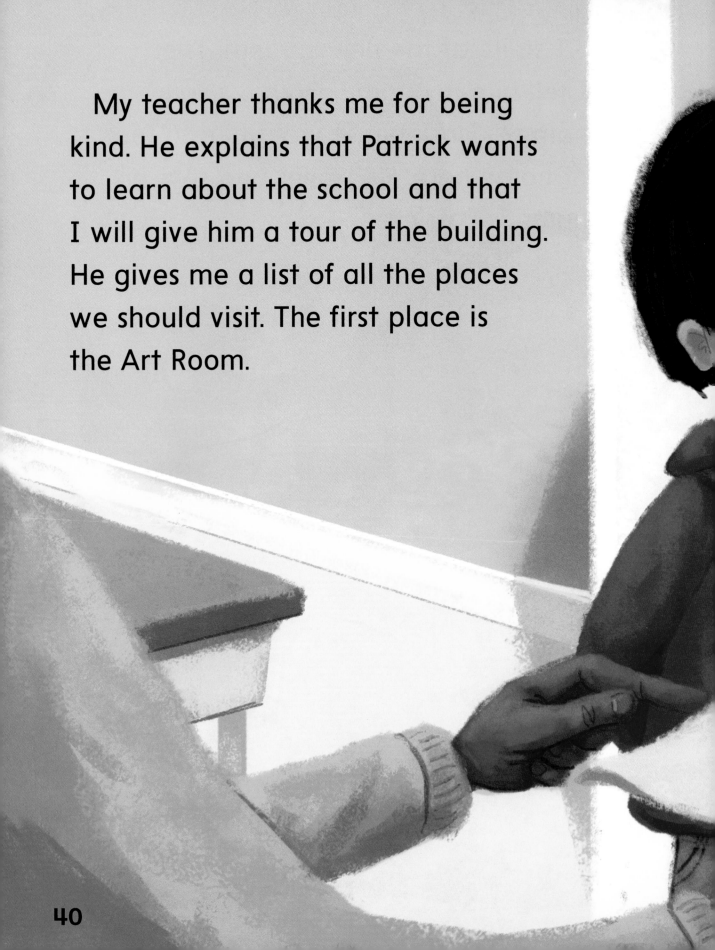

My teacher thanks me for being kind. He explains that Patrick wants to learn about the school and that I will give him a tour of the building. He gives me a list of all the places we should visit. The first place is the Art Room.

Art Room

Patrick and I step into the Art Room.
On the door we see the letters A, R,
and T. I show him the work tables.

Then we look at the supplies. I show
him the paper and crayons. I point to
the paint and brushes. I tell Patrick
that art class is fun. He tells me that
he likes to draw pictures. I like to do
that, too!

Music Room

Next we walk to the Music Room. We say hello to the music teacher. She shows us a few instruments that we will play in class. Patrick smiles and says he likes music a lot.

Lunch Room

We walk into the empty lunchroom. It is too early for lunch. I remember how confusing lunchtime was at first. I tell Patrick, "You can sit with me at lunch. I will introduce you to my friends." He smiles and responds, "Thank you! I would like that."

The Library

The next place is my favorite of all. It is the library! Shelves fill the room with rows and rows of books. I remind Patrick to whisper. It is story time now and a class is listening to the librarian read aloud.

I show Patrick where he can find lots of picture books. Some are about animals. Some are fairy tales. As we leave, he tells me, "The library is my favorite room."

Our Classroom

We both return to our classroom. I point out where we sit when we read stories. I show him the jars of beans and flashcards we use for adding and subtracting during math.

Patrick thanks me for showing him the school. I smile and say, "You're welcome!"

My teacher is writing spelling words on the board. The first one is "friend."

I smile and look at Patrick. He smiles back at me. It is good to have a new friend.

Can you trace the path these students took in the school?

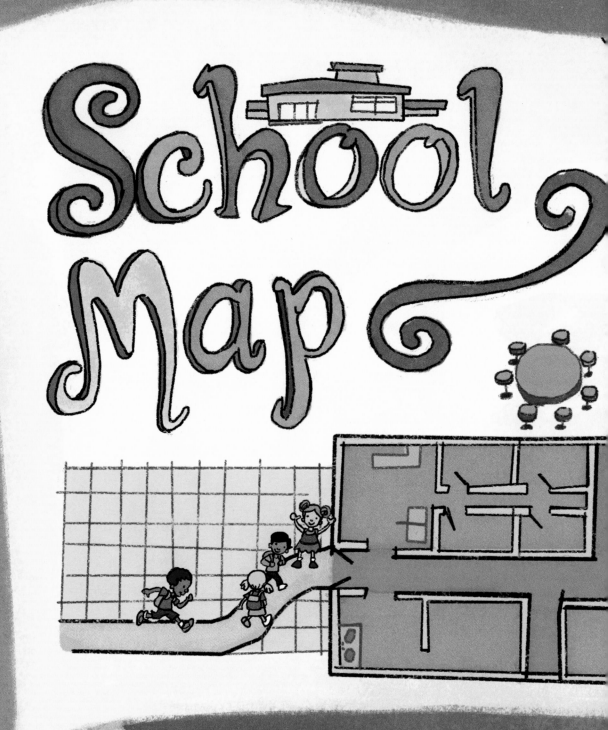

Glossary

A

act
to behave in a particular way

again
once more

around
to different parts of an area

C

confusing
a form of the verb
confuse: mixed up

F

fair
treating people equally or the same

I

introduce
to make known

M

minute
a unit of time equal
to sixty seconds

P

poor
a form of the verb
poor: unlucky

R

**rather (would
rather)**
instead of; prefer

S

stinks
to be very
unpleasant,
unfair, etc.

T

too
more than enough

tour
going from place
to place to see and
learn about the
different parts

trace
to follow or track